# RUIN & BEAUTY

# RUIN & BEAUTY

NEW AND SELECTED POEMS

# PATRICIA YOUNG

Published in 2000 by
House of Anansi Press Limited
34 Lesmill Road
Toronto, ON M3B 2T6
Tel. (416) 445-3333
Fax (416) 445-5967
www.anansi.ca

Distributed in Canada by
General Distribution Services Ltd.
325 Humber College Blvd.
Etobicoke, ON M9W 7C3
Tel. (416) 213-1919
Fax (416) 213-1917
E-mail cservice@genpub.com

04 03 02 01 00    1 2 3 4 5

CANADIAN CATALOGUING IN PUBLICATION DATA

Young, Patricia, 1954–
Ruin & beauty: new and selected poems

ISBN 0-88784-649-1

I. Title II. Ruin and beauty.

PS8597.O673R84 2000    C811'.54    C00-930076-7
PR9199.3.Y68R84 2000

Cover design: Angel Guerra
Typesetting: Brian Panhuyzen
Printed and bound in Canada

THE CANADA COUNCIL | LE CONSEIL DES ARTS
FOR THE ARTS | DU CANADA
SINCE 1957 | DEPUIS 1957

*We acknowledge for their financial support of our publishing program the Canada
Council for the Arts, the Ontario Arts Council, and the Government of Canada
through the Book Publishing Industry Development Program (BPIDP).*

*This book is for Clea and Liam.*

# Contents

## How Mysterious the World Was

## Travelling the Floodwaters

## Melancholy Ain't No Baby

## The Mad and Beautiful Mothers

## Those Were the Mermaid Days

## More Watery Still

## What I Remember from My Time on Earth

How Mysterious the World Was

# Ruin and Beauty

It's so quiet now the children have decided to stop
being born. We raise our cups in an empty room.
In this light, the curtains are transparent as gauze.
Through the open window we hear nothing —
no airplane, lawn mower, no siren
speeding its white pain through the city's traffic.
There is no traffic. What remains is all that remains.

The brick school at the five points crosswalk
is drenched in morning glory.
Its white flowers are trumpets
festooning this coastal town.
Will the eventual forest rise up
and remember our footsteps? Already
seedlings erupt through cement,
crabgrass heaves through cracked marble,
already wolves come down from the hills
to forage among us. We are like them now,
just another species looking to the stars
and howling extinction.

They say the body accepts any kind of sorrow,
that our ancestors lay down on their stomachs
in school hallways, as children they lay down
like matches waiting for a nuclear fire.

It wasn't supposed to end like this:
all ruin and beauty, vines waterfalling down
a century's architecture; it wasn't supposed to end
so quietly, without fanfare or fuss,

a man and woman collecting rain
in old coffee tins. Darling,
the wars have been forgotten.
These days our quarrels are only with ourselves.
Tonight you sit on the edge of the bed loosening your shoes.
The act is soundless, without future
weight. Should we name this failure?
Should we wake to the regret at the end of time
doing what people have always done
and say it was not enough?

## Elephants
1992, Acrylic on Wood 8' x 4'


First we saw nothing and then they were feeding on thornscrub
outside our bedroom door; we saw their domed heads,
their knees sinking into the mud.

In the flushed country of sleep what else did we see —
termite mounds rising from the iron-rich earth?

We had no reason to wake.
Swallows wove around us, egrets
perched on the banister and lamps.

Do I need to remind you? We also had
telephones, garbage collection, bills to pay,
time enough to make ponderous love.

Those hot summer nights we lay on our backs,
sheet pushed to the floor. They say a lost migratory route
will lead to springwater, that even in dreams
you can hear the drumbeat of rain.

To think. For years we walked up the stairs
seeing nothing — no swamp-dwelling antelope arching its back,
no lowland gorilla thumping its chest.
We'd stop on the landing waiting for sunlight
to crash through monocot leaves.

And when we woke, what did we wake to,
what hacked-off tusks, what severed trunk?
Heat pressed against our guts like poachers' fists,

we sank beneath the weight of all that lustrous dentine.
We looked at each other and knew what we were—
fingers, thumb, a convoluted brain.

Tonight, I'm standing outside our bedroom door.

The jungle's splashed like blood against the wall.
I can hear you moving through the house,
turning out lights. I don't need to tell you
how rank the colours—yellow fig,
blue mango, red treetops wrapped in liana.

But I will say this—
first there was nothing and then
great living things came down to drink.

# Driving Down the Amalfi Coast

*For the people of Amalfi who go to heaven, the day of judgement*
*will be just like any other day.*
—Renato Fucini


Ryan Schmitke's at the wheel of the little red coupe;
there is no other word to describe the car in which we find ourselves
this summer afternoon. The narrow road
hugs a cliff face but he drives
crazed as any Italian, bumper-to-bumper,
darting out
to pass
despite the sharp
turns — the rock wall on one side,
                                    breathtaking
                plunge
on the other. There's been nothing
between us since the afternoon we winked
through a class detention, winked
happily at each other
out the corners of our eyes,
hands behind backs, ankles shackled to our desks.

Our lives since then —
the marriages, children, deaths —
seem to have
                plummeted
into the turquoise sea. At least
that's what I'm thinking when Ryan Schmitke steps on the gas,
leans forward, bunching up his bony shoulders.

He glances over, grinning like a ten-year-old,
and I am moved almost to tears:
that I am hurtling along
one of the earth's most beautiful coastlines
with a boy utterly unspoiled

by time. With each twist in the road
the world beyond the car window
swells up like the blue
that fills the swimmer's brain
and I tell him

I have loved him all these years, since the day
Miss Horner stepped out of the classroom
at Quadra Elementary to take a phone call.
But he is shaking his head, he can't remember
the spring morning the entire fifth grade
erupted into a spontaneous riot
of flinging chalk. If only

I could convince him
this is how it was meant to be—
the two of us strapped into seat belts
with only our eyes to carry the light—
I know our separate pasts
would scatter behind us
like the pink and yellow cottages
clumped around
each passing harbour.

## How Mysterious the World Was

In the caves of Lascaux there's a painting of a human
body with the head of a bird. A lanky
Frenchman tells us this in the summer of 1974.
My sister and I know nothing
of the Paleolithic period or the boys
who entered the Shaft of the Dead Man
in the early forties searching for their lost dog.

Travelling around Europe, we've stumbled by accident
upon a world-famous site, its unique cave art.
We're hot and thirsty and dragging
our knapsacks through another train station
when the man tells us
there've been no tourist excursions
into the caves for over ten years
but what luck
he's an archaeologist with a key to their entrance.

He leads us up the side of a hill, down through a tunnel,
then lights a candle. How long
do my sister and I stand in that cavern of silence
watching bears and wolves flicker on walls,
before we're struck by our monumental
stupidity — following a stranger
into the earth's fungal depths?

But the archaeologist is kind.
His arms sweep about his head as though
the vaulted roof were painted yesterday
just for our pleasure. In broken English

he tries to explain the red and yellow pigments,
how mysterious the world was to those who engraved
the animals and latticelike signs.

Before leaving, I pull out my camera,
ask him to take our picture. Beside the beautiful
small horses we pose as ourselves.

On the walk back to town
the archaeologist is particularly attentive
to my sister, keeps reaching
for her hand. I drop behind, pretending
not to listen: he's asking her back to the caves
the next day, he wants
to take some photographs of his own —
my sister against the polychrome walls
painted seventeen thousand years ago.
This time without clothes.

*As if*, she groans later in bed,
wondering
what it would be like
to lie naked in that prehistoric dark —
a wounded bison frozen above her, a hunter
kneeling to drink of her body.

# The Clyde

In Scotland, where the boys stand on the banks,
poles jutting upwards, lures dangling
like silver tongues, the girls
are mostly named Margaret.

I served fish and chips in stiff newspaper cones.
All evening those boys came in for soft drinks
and mushy peas, their faces caught
between childhood and the heavy years ahead.

If I stood by a window
I could see light pass through my dark ribs.
If I spoke three times
I could hear what was beautiful:
*The river rises in the highland moors, the river rises*
*in the highland etc.*

Mother polished her brasses on the front stoop,
candlesticks, plates, little men in kilts.
Behind her on the table: the King James Bible,
its onionskin pages open to Lamentations.
When she rubbed those dull ornaments
I knew He was close, as close as the closest
bridge spanning the water.

On Fridays Father came home from the sugar factory
with a tinful of broken candy. *Oh my papa,*
*to me he was so wonderful, oh my papa,*
*to me he was so good. . .*

. . . how did I get here, down at the dockyard, the stink
of creosote and fish guts, a boy from the river
moving his hands clumsily inside my jacket?
I close my eyes and his mouth—

till now, mute or incomprehensible —
is suddenly not a mouth at all.
*Och Maggie*, he says, puzzled as anyone.

Dead thirty years
and his voice
can still strip my bones clean.

## Pantoum to a Dead Husband

It rained the day you swam in the canal with the local boys.
They said the water was the cleanest on earth.
Soon after we left that Balkan town there was war.
All month the hours moved through our hands like river stones.

They said the water was the cleanest on earth.
Beneath the hotel a wine cellar had been blasted out of rock.
All month the hours moved through our hands like river stones.
How the waiters glowered pouring chicory coffee before dawn.

Beneath the hotel a wine cellar had been blasted out of rock.
It was August, the newspapers said nothing.
How the waiters glowered pouring chicory coffee before dawn.
Walking the streets was like following a long, slow thought.

It was August, the newspapers said nothing.
After dark folksingers performed in the square.
Walking the streets was like following a long, slow thought.
Songs we didn't understand made grown men weep.

After dark folksingers performed in the square.
Beneath our window a woman kept wringing her hands.
Songs we didn't understand made grown men weep.
I remember the sun glowed like a blood orange over the lake.

Beneath our window a woman kept wringing her hands.
It was long ago; the country was destroyed.
I remember the sun glowed like a blood orange over the lake.
Why am I telling you this?

It was long ago; the country was destroyed.
Soon after we left that Balkan town there was war.
Why am I telling you this?
That it rained the day you swam in the canal with the local boys?

## Settebello

Let us not forget the day we rented lounge chairs
and a blue *ombrello* beneath which we read
fat, American novels. All that shiftlessness
just metres from a pounding sea.
Beside us, three generations of Italians
picnicked in shade they'd also purchased
earlier that morning from a young man
who marched across the beach
in the first light of dawn to set up business.
Let us not forget the outdoor showers, those metal stems
that seemed to sprout like gushing periscopes
in a desert of sand or the gypsy boy
permitted briefly into the cordoned-off area
of reclining sunbathers to hawk his wares —
the long cotton scarves wrapped
around his waist and neck so that he looked
like a bored and lavishly dressed god
moving among the indolent damned.
And the yellow dress
draped across his outstretched arms
as though he were carrying from family to family
the body of someone who'd departed
the earth just moments before. Who
would claim it as one of their own?
A dress so transparent in the Mediterranean light
that it opened several dozing women's eyes,
pushing the women up on their elbows
to run the cloth through their fingers.
Let us not forget that boy's face
as he stumbled toward us, speaking a flattened
English, *Do you want to buy, do you want
to buy?* No one did
on that sweltering afternoon
at the end of which his father drove into the hotel

parking lot in an aging Mercedes.
By then we were sitting on the veranda, stupid
with sun and heat, lemon gelato melting in our mouths,
while on the hilltop behind us a white statue
of Christ — thirty gleaming metres high —
looked down on a man
unwinding his son's dark body.

# Music Lesson

On Friday afternoons we sang like mad —
*Hang down your head Tom Dooley,*
*Hang down your head and cry.*

We'd never heard anything
as beautiful as the sound of our own voices.

Mr. Brown taught us to harmonize
The Kingston Trio's version

(though there are others
in which Tom buries a girl named Laura Foster
on a North Carolina hillside then stomps
her body down).

Look at those children
sitting on top of their desks, riding
the tilted platforms as though riding surfboards.

Try telling a class full of nine-year-olds a man will murder
for love.

Back then we didn't know Tennessee
was a place on the map; it was simply the high note we fled to.

But we knew the wide oak tree from which hunted men swung.
Walked through our own wooded grove
on the way home from school.

(In autumn, those fallen leaves
were slices of brown bread and we,
busy housewives, made moss sandwiches
for our imaginary husbands to eat
during their imaginary lunch breaks
down at the dry dock.)

Sure, Tom met her on the mountain;
sure, he stabbed her with a knife. But it was June.
A warm salt wind blew off the sea,
our teacher ambled up and down the aisles
strumming his guitar and looking
like Paul Anka. It was Mr. Brown
strolling past my desk, necktie pulled loose,
and smelling of aftershave. O Lord,
I threw back my head —

*Poor boy you're bound to die.*

# Feast

They say the brain is designed to comprehend
a world of medium-sized objects
moving in three dimensions
at moderate speeds. I
could do that, I could understand
a man's body swinging through a kitchen,

roll my face across a fridge door, glower at crabs
being dropped into boiling water.

What an odd thing to be a child.
Not to know the names of things
or that a planet is dying beneath your feet—
leopards, oak trees, marbled murrelets.

Cheek pressed against a cool surface,
I could see tongs lift hard pink bodies
out of a pot, hear walls shudder relief.

*Trust me, they can't feel, they aren't even fish,*
my father called behind, already down
the back steps, cracking legs open
as though they were Christmas nuts.

If I could return to my life
the way some people return from death
I'd see a man and child sitting on upturned buckets,
a newspaper spread like a tablecloth between them.

What an odd thing not to care that you evolved
from a spineless sea creature but now walk upright.
Not to understand the word *crustacean*,
but to know flesh as food, an ocean
sloshing within the flask of your skin.

## Smelter Town

On Friday afternoons the wooden sidewalks ran
into the Skeena River.
It was no joke. We were pear trees
struggling to bloom in snow.

There was a garden party, our mother
in a short green jacket, my sisters and I
gobbling dainty sandwiches.
Though it was lonely
eating under the kitchen table,
the thin singing
of a mosquito trapped in my ear.

Face to face with my sisters' scabbed knees
and my mother's slippers,
I couldn't think —
what herb
had been left out of the soup?

And yes
it's odd that people behave so badly
toward their own children.

There goes my father with his cowlick bangs.
Forty years have passed since he worked in the smelter.
What more can I tell you about that aluminum town?
That all the streets were named Pheasant
or Partridge or Swan?

That one summer night
my mother lay on the driveway
so my father couldn't leave?

My sister also lay down and closed her eyes.
She must have been six when she said
with conviction, *I know who I am,*

her words drawing me up to the top
bunk where I sat on her stomach and pried
her lids open. *Who, who?* I demanded
like a terrible bird.

## Staccato Punch

Thank God for the bully who hunted me down
each morning of winter, thank God
he shoved my face in the snow.
Who would I be
if his boots hadn't padded
softly behind me, his taunts
descending from one of the Mediterranean tongues.

You know how it goes.
Someone small and ridiculous
tumbles down the porch steps stuffed in a snowsuit.
In thin northern light: a sitting duck, blinking target.
I thought no one could see me if I stayed very still.

They say one person's helplessness
calls out to another's cruelty like the call of a lover.
What does a victim know of its tormentor?
Mine had no name or address, jeered
in Portuguese, Greek, or Italian.

If you've studied nature
you know anything alive can turn
suddenly dangerous. A day in early spring
when I swung round like a boxer,
threw a jab at his cheek.

Watch
as he falls
in slow
motion, back-

wards into the snow-
bank. The drip of icicles
melting from eaves, his breath
as he flails like something broken.

I'm told the women came out of their houses,
cardigans pulled tight around their shoulders,
that they cheered to see the boy,
bloody and sobbing, the staccato
punch of the girl's fist, I'm told
there's a message
that travels to the brain
that says, *Enough, stop,*
but
I did not hear it.

# South Fairfield, Number 6

She sidles down the aisle,
music books held close to her body.
A dull axe slams into his chest.

The girl sits by the rear door and he leans forward,
hissing something insulting and full
of desire. They say

a millennium of light drifted over the grasslands.
What connection
between those acres of heat
and the boy's pupils
floating in his sockets like black moons?

Beginning of winter:
a girl travelling home for dinner.
As always, a boy somewhere close by.

She swivels round on the torn leather seat,
sees his eyes brimming with something
he longs to give her
though he doesn't know what.

In the optometrist's office,
insects crawled over the medical charts.
Now the streetlights hurt his head.

Earlier, the girl's music teacher said:
*I'm leaving for London to study opera.*
Side by side on the piano bench
they stared at the keys. And then
the girl played badly: Chopin's Waltz in E Minor.

When the doctor unrolled the alphabet
jabbing at this and that with a wooden pointer

the boy understood the man
was just trying to be kind.

He looks at the back of the girl's head
wanting the thud inside his body
to mean more than these streets
and all their reasons —

the bus carrying its load
past the clock tower,
its bells ringing the darkness in.

# Overdose

*Tomorrow I might lie beneath a ton of rubble*
*but right now I am infinitely incorruptible,* he said at fifteen,
the drug overtaking him. I was wearing blue
seersucker, the dress
my mother'd sewn at the kitchen table.

Like every new couple
we were already squeezing
the life out of each other.

There are gaps in my memory,
a few that sound like the names of birds.
People in that town were always in a flap
over some rare sighting. Even the trees
waved their brilliant plumage
the day we stood on the church steps,
wanting a ride, thumbs testing the wind.

Later, sitting on the bed in my basement room,
he rubbed his chin like a serious old man
with something serious to say:
*I want to go clean.* I stood back
as though surveying a charred land, while my mother,
singing above us, seared small chunks of beef in a cast-iron pan.

Did she imagine we were bent over homework,
stuck on a difficult equation?

By seventeen he was dead.

If only he'd stop appearing on the back step, a stoned boy
in an open-necked shirt. As usual, his body is haloed in light.
If only I could turn from where he stands in the doorway,
look down at my mother's hair falling in waves
across sunburned shoulders. As she kneels
at my knees, mouth full of pins.

# Drunk

I knew what I had to do when I saw him
lurching toward me across the lawn.
*Mend the hole in my heart*, he might have sung
to the wild geese flying over our heads.
I felt for his keys in my back pocket.
His wife, that lovely Scottish girl,
stood in front of the Valiant,
arms crossed like a prison guard's.
And when he tripped over his feet,
the stiff fingers of the wind
caught him before he fell. It was late
and the children peered out the rear window.
I could see it in his eyes: nothing would stop him.
He *would* drive that car down the starlit
highway, he loved those kids so much
he *would* stumble deeper
and deeper into the broken world.
*Dae it, dae it*, the woman shouted at me,
her dress stained with blueberries,
the hopeless future careening toward her.
Was it good advice? I don't know
but a fist swam out of my sleeve and he fell to the ground.
I might have said, *Brother, let's sit on the grass
and talk of those long afternoons
we cast our lines into the river*, I might have
kissed his forehead before knocking him
out cold, I might have turned
to the children who for years afterwards
would roll their eyes, the whites
whiter than the white of a hooked fish belly.

# Earwig

*Once thought to enter the head through the ear.*
— Concise Oxford Dictionary


This morning I bring one in with a handful of pears.
I shake my wrist, it drops into the sink.
*Are you just going to let it suffer?*
my son asks, watching the struggle
in sudsy water. *I hate them,* I say,
turning my back while he scoops the drowned
slip of a creature onto a plate and takes it outside.

The story I've told him seems not to matter:
the night my sister woke screaming, our parents away.
How she pressed her hand over her ear
trying to shut out the pain while I stood by
helpless. And when an insect finally emerged —
its horrible sheen and pincer like forceps — I squeezed
its life between my fingers. *Evil,* I say to my son,

*I have seen its size and shape, it is*
*a small centipede drilling into the drum's*
*delicate nerve, I have seen it*
*crawl out of the body's chamber and pause*
*at the entrance: a torturer*
*grown bored*
*with his own dark ministrations.*

## For Years She Fell

In the other room my daughter is cursing in her sleep.
*Daughter*, I ask, *what troubles your heart in the dead of night?*
She picks up a ukulele and strums "Way Over Jordan Lord"
but it does not help. The walls around her bed
keep falling down. She curses
the day she was born, her little room beneath the stairs.
Just three days old when I pushed her bassinet
to the front of the hospital,
into that glassed-in
sunroom full of swollen women.
But there was no sun; rain blistered the sheets of glass.

What do I mean when I say I lifted her out,
swaddled and yellow-faced, carried her to an open window,
when I say she slipped from my hands? *It was only*
*a dream*, I tell my daughter, *just like the dream*
*of billy goats stampeding above your head.*

I stand in the doorway trying to decipher her words.
How impossible they are, each one's a misshapen stutter
the mind cannot follow. Again and again
I was drawn to that window,
and when I let go
the baby fell, for years
she fell out of my body until now when I must speak
to these curses in the dead of night.

*Let me write your words down,*
I say to my daughter, *we can solve them in the morning.*
*Let me tell you about Julie, the farm girl*
*who walked three rural kilometres to visit her best friend*
*one last time before moving to the city.*
*How she took her little brother*
*and a bag of their clothes.* Think

of Julie's mother finding the girl's pyjama bottoms
caught on a bush, saddling her horse,
charging through the maple trees.

See those children walking into a hayfield,
past grazing deer, crossing two wooden bridges
until they arrive on the friend's porch
where their mother finally finds them.

My daughter in the other room says,
*I love that story, the little girl and her brother*
*leaving a trail of socks and T-shirts*
*like pebbles or crumbs.*

## Still Life: Trout on a Plate
## Bordered with Sunflowers

I knew nothing, truly.
About the trout my son caught at the lake.

For years, he'd been a strict vegetarian.
It was the first catch of his life.

That day I walked along the old train tracks
while he stood on a rock casting through the long afternoon.

Back home, he measured in centimetres.
On the bathroom scales it was just over a half-kilo.

I had come to think of my son as you'd think
of an animal: silent, hungry, terribly alive.

This is a fish story to which I can add very little.
Except that a boy stood at a kitchen sink

watching his father slide a knife through a trout's belly.
The day was a gutting and cleaning.

He was my son but what did I know.
At fourteen he refused to put meat into his mouth.

Later there were dinner guests.
Who they were I couldn't say; their faces elude me.

As for the fish, it was fried in butter,
garlic, a little white wine.

How the guests praised my son
as the plate moved around the table.

Also the trout for swimming into his bait.
In the end there was enough to feed everyone.

Some meals are like that, beyond understanding.
In general, what I know is of no use.

Like the dead eye of a fish
surrounded by yellow flowers.

## Why the Juniper Rushed In

I taught my daughter nothing but the trees,
the great cedars and pines taught her to carve
the air between words. Did I teach her to swim,

did I hold her thin flashing body in an upturned hand?
No, the poplars bent down at the edge of the lake
and said: *Like this* and *Like this*. Where had I gone

the day she took a mug of tea to drink among the alders?
I saw her coming out of the forest, a sock monkey over an arm.
No credit to me for her grace or way with the animals.

The maples taught her to stitch these thick orange gloves.
Was I scrubbing the bathtub, sick with flu
when the aspens rattled their bracelets

and my daughter went running? The fruit trees
must have told her the sounds to bring down the birds.
If I taught her anything, it was impatience, to keep

the floors clean. I understand a tree is not an ox
or electricity, it is not the sonata she played the evening
I stood in the driveway, the windows all open.

In those days a sequoia towered above the neighbourhood.
My daughter was only nine but already her name
in my mouth was the taste of old grief. They say

childhood leaves scars on the brain just as it leaves
scars on the body. So I thank the hard oaks. Without
their furrowed bark she could not have survived.

# Château de Cheverny

Nothing's prepared her for this green and heavy morning
in which she finds herself wandering the private
apartments of dead aristocrats. Above,
a three-year-old boy dressed in full armour
floats in and out of doorways. In the Loire valley,
in the ancestral home of the Huraults,
family of financiers and officers, my daughter
sighs beneath the weight of that clanking cherub,
the shadow of a future falling across her face.

It is hot inside the king's bedroom
but she shivers in a sleeveless dress.
Here is Persian silk draped around a four-poster bed
but where are the stitches
that make up the embroidered forest
that is her life? She sighs and so do the Louis xiv
armchairs, so does the sideboard built by an artisan from Blois.

She sighs at the child sliding down the limestone
balustrade carved from the River Cher,
at the Japanese tourist entering the small boudoir,
the French guide who bends slightly from the waist,
clipping his heels together and wanting her to love,
as he loves, the writing desk signed by Stockel,
cabinetmaker to Marie Antoinette.

If a sigh could be interpreted, if it could unravel its meaning
like a seventeenth-century tapestry —

Helen stepping from a beached boat,
looking over her shoulder at Paris, prince of Troy.

When all else fails my daughter draws air
into her lungs and slowly exhales. And why not
in a trophy room decked out with two thousand antlers?

I stand on the stone steps, watching her walk across the lawns.
Even from this distance I can see her shoulders
rise and fall as though she's already decided
how pointless a life can be. Oh, her sighing
wears me out, it backs me
up against the wall, I
do not understand the forlorn thing
she does with her body or why she stops before the pack
of caged thoroughbreds, no, I do not understand
those seventy foxhounds turning their heads
in her direction or how a girl's sigh
can bear down on the earth
like the smell of an animal
cornered in the hunt.

# The Unidentified Child

Beneath the newspaper's headlines
an unidentified child
appears among the murdered girl's family.

Her face floats
between the mother and father's elbows
as though guiding the grieving parents
through the crowd. Who is she —
family friend, acquaintance, stray
child come in off the street?

Her presence in the midst of front-page tragedy is pure
as an ice cube. I close my eyes;
she melts beneath my lids.

All over the city we are bending over the welcome
mats on our porches. It's a balmy day
in December; we don't want to read
of bones being broken under a bridge.
Don't want to see the heron's slow flight
over the gorge, a girl floating face down.

And what will the unidentified child remember
of the day of the funeral —
TV cameras, flashing lights?
What will she remember of the night
that followed the day — the city's mauve skyline,
light streaming from a corner store,
her stiff cotton dress hanging
straight on her body?

Did she step out of the photograph
to eat at a fast-food restaurant, did she

and her brother sit in a booth
playing the table between them
as though a drum?

This morning the unidentified child holds
our attention then lets it go. She's the kind
to slosh miles in the ankle-deep sea,
sand dollars in her pockets.
Already she is growing away from us.
One day she'll trail boys, her lips
will go soft learning desire.

## The Place Children Go

After the funeral we walk beneath the flowering trees.
As if trying to prevent the stuffing from falling out of our bodies.

We didn't know the man well though we knew him well enough
to be saddened by his leaving. Some die. Others keep living.

They buy groceries, chop vegetables, eat the next meal.
At the funeral I couldn't hear what the man's friends

were saying at the front of the room so I watched his son.
Not older than twelve — blue eyes, red hair, white shirt, and tie.

He looked as any boy looks in his Sunday best — restless,
uncomfortable, he looked like a boy dragged to some dull,

adult affair, and told to be still, told to listen. But he was not
listening. He shifted from foot to foot, eyes coming back

to the table spread with cream cakes and brownies.
Whatever the man's friends said about his father

he did not hear it. In that room crowded with memory
and loss he stood like someone gone into himself. Gone

to that place children go to when the life that was their life
has walked out the house and shut the back door.

## True to Their Living Selves

Last summer two old friends died by drowning.
The incidents were separate,
they occurred in different waters.

A beachcomber looking through binoculars
thought he saw a seal bobbing off the coast or was it
a woman's head? By then it was too late.

Twice she'd walked into the waves to the sound
of her mother calling, twice the Coast Guard
had scooped her out of the sea. We'd known

the other since he was almost a boy.
The kind to climb a mountain face
despite a wood-chip path up the other side.

He lived in his flesh with an abandon we half condemned,
half admired. On a family vacation the morning
he dove off a cliff into a river pool.

They say he emerged briefly, smiled and waved
to his daughter watching from above.
Later his body was found downstream.

At the funeral I didn't ask if there was a reason.
An undercurrent? Did he hit his head,
what took him for its own dark purposes?

There is nothing beautiful to say about drowning
though in dreams my friends rise up and speak,
a watery light around the kitchen table.

## Open House

Walking back from the beach I saw a sign on the front lawn.
It was a cottage. And nothing had changed.
A real estate agent was sweeping
bits of broken sea glass out the back door.
Many fear death and I did too.
Everything was as I remembered it from childhood.
Even the little framed birds on the walls.
Even the ridiculous dog, her fluffy coat,
the streaks of a wolfhound. I knew the names
of all the irises in my mother's front beds.
In the entrance, a garish chandelier swung above my head.
It was a yappy toy Pomeranian.
Words startle up when I say them out loud —
*yappy, ridiculous*. Odd, considering the pride
with which I carried that dog everywhere.
Tiny thoroughbred, runt of the litter.
When I put her down she'd gallop ahead
on the sidewalk, sideways like a crab.
The real estate agent had no voice.
Despite this, she led me through the rooms
explaining their unique, cobalt features.
The building's design allowed for a different phase
of the moon to shine through each window.
When I was a girl, that dog lived in the crook of my arm.
Wet, she was the size of a rat.
All our lives the dead say nothing and no wonder.
If I acquire a taste for prayer, I'll pray for the inbred
animals: *Lord, give them the strength*.
What I loved about that dog was the innocence.
At the end of her life you could look in her eyes
and see she'd learned nothing.

## Marriage: The First Year

She can't sleep. He can't stay awake.
It's been like this for months now.
Since the elopement and field mice
dropped out of the sagging rose wallpaper.
She's peeling logs. He's building an outhouse.
They won't last, you can see they won't make it.
There's no electricity, there's no well.
She's pacing the porch, his eyes are shut.
They sit in the hole he dug before hitting bedrock.
From one minute to the next
they don't know what they're thinking.
It's spring, he's asleep in the forest, his mouth's full of clay.
She lays a fire. Not carefully, not the way
he's shown her, a perfect little pyramid.
It's baked potatoes again, it's black peas and cod.
His face is starved as a dinner plate, her skin is tea-stained.
They hold onto each other, they let go.
He fills the kerosene lamps, she wipes the glass chimneys.
There are thunderstorms, there are skunk
cabbages, an oak barrel collecting run-off rain.
She rides her bike into the city, fumes in the library,
reading yesterday's newspapers. He lies down
in a wrought-iron bed. Somewhere on the Aegean
his old girlfriend sails a small wooden boat.
They are weeping, they are shouting,
they are hanging Pablo Neruda out to dry.
You can see it won't last. She buries
her head in his unwashed clothes,
he brings home lemons, a bottle of gin.
In a room above the kitchen they sweat it out,
blind to what's coming: bulldozers
and chainsaws, deer

standing in open spaces. She
is spitting up dirt, he
feels the foundation about to give away.
They reach out in the dark. Hands
like labourers, like technicians, like apricot pickers.

# Narcoleptic

Evelyn's Croatian lover
sits on her steps, smoking Gauloises.
Today he has a helper, an apprentice

who's come to learn the art
of smoothing plaster
over the bones of a small wooden house.

Summer begins. All over the city
birds fall out of trees.
In the front yard a ginger cat

circles a bunch of feathered quivering.
I want to help. But the hysterical
parents, their frantic swooping!

Wings slice past my head,
razor-bright and almost
as threatening. When the cigarettes

run out, the Croatian nods his head.
The apprentice roars off in a truck,
returns to mix sand and lye and water.

All morning the Croatian's trowel
moves over the tawny surface
of Evelyn's house

as though over a woman's skin.
There's an effect he's trying to achieve —
a five-hundred-year-old cottage

in Brittany. The Croatian might not
be Evelyn's lover. He might be the first
stonemason she flipped to

in the yellow pages
after returning from France.
When I move too close

the bird hops across the lawn —
a mutant frog with no pond
to slide into. Now the Croatian

is back on the scaffolding
clenching his teeth, now his eyelids
are dark blinds sliding down.

## Sex Is like Geologic Time

People will tell you they married for love
and I've said that too but now
I'm too old for such lies.
I've seen it all —
the terrible bodies slammed together
in dust. What we're made of
spins us together —
churning things
that assume
a single, disc-like shape.
And when pieces break off
and become planets,
parts of ourselves
cool in the distance.

At eighteen I crouched above him
and it was like looking into eons
of fog. I couldn't see past
my shrinking self. Or was I
expanding? And always the hammering
of meteorites, craters being blasted
out of molten rock, oh, he was
a boy with lofty ideas
but I kept rising up beside him
all water and hunger.

We didn't notice plants and animals
beginning to appear, we were too busy
sliding belly against belly. Ah,
the pact to be true. Who were we kidding?
The body springs from the earth,
untameable as the grasses.

If I showed you things sped-up —
seas swamping deserts
then draining away, mountains erupting
and wearing down, species
becoming extinct or evolving
into new forms — you'd see what I saw
looking down from our unmade bed,
you'd see the North and South Poles
wandering like nomads
for somewhere solid to dig in their heels.

When I was young
I didn't know what it meant —
I looked in his eyes and saw continents
drifting away from a single landmass, my legs
were always buckling beneath me,
I didn't understand sex
is like geologic time, and change
so gradual you can only see it
if you look back
over your shoulder.

## My New Blond Husband

Just three weeks since we'd gone to city hall and said I do.
I didn't have a summer job so my parents,
thinking I was still a daughter, said,
*There's room in the car, why not come along?*
A week at a lakeside cabin, swimming
with my younger sisters, barbecues at night.
On the second morning I was as surprised as anyone
when I woke up, arms and legs aching.
My sisters laughed and said it must be for him,
my new blond husband, and I laughed too,
but at the end of the week, sick with a fever
I didn't understand, I guessed something
of the body's deep unravelling.
Driving home through the mountains
I kept looking over my father's shoulder,
begging him to go faster. By then,
my bones, muscles, even my blood
wailed for an end to it. I closed my eyes
to make time speed up, opened them
to highways twisting and turning
like the pins falling from my mother's hair.
On the ferry, gulls hung above the deck furniture,
trapped inside pockets of air. And then
the kilometres of dirt road to the cabin
we'd moved into after the makeshift wedding.
He heard the car, was waiting at the gate
when we rounded the last bend.
We didn't touch, just stood facing each other
while my father, already backing up, turned toward the city.
I don't know who he saw all those years ago
but I saw a boy in a faded denim workshirt,
a boy with tanned skin and cheekbones
high and chiselled as a Cherokee's. Time
passed and still we didn't move, weakness

rising up in us like a kind a beauty. That
was all I wanted: to look in silence, to be one of those people
who travel the world to stand beneath a tree,
eyes fixed on a rare bird. It seemed a good way
to spend a life — feet on the ground,
hands at the sides, all of me taking him in.

## Red Tide, 1966

Alone in my room I groped the air.
It was a blindfolded game I played to get back
to my plankton beginnings.
First there were children
clambering over rocks
and then there was blooming
algae. The days were long and light
just as they were at the dawn of time —
microscopic organisms drifting in warm
waves, great numbers drifting near the surface . . .
Foolish to spend Saturday nights reaching for walls
that might not be there. I am sorry
for what I've written; it's a salty mess
concentrated in the photic zone.
*No mussels tonight*, Mother said, *give back
the screwdrivers*. That summer,
unblossomed cells
blossomed in the tideless air.
It's why children often stopped
in the shadow
of the valley of death
before moving on down the beach.
In all the world I could not sleep.
Not while the dead sandpiper opened its beak.
Invertebrates and fish also littered the sand.
The girls said things like: *Light is absorbed as it penetrates water.*
*Who cares*, the boys answered, tumbling
happily to the bottom of the food chain.
It is late in life to walk into the sea
as though walking into
the flowering rye at the end of the street
but here I go —
waist, shoulders, the swallowed-
up head.

# Raising Alexandria

I watched them dive down, attaching obelisks and bas-reliefs
to balloons filled with compressed air.
Once inflated, the relics floated to the surface
like lost toys in a swimming pool.
The words *algae* and *seashell* had not encrusted my tongue.
It was before I understood you could lose love
over no one special, for nothing
lasting to speak of, that you could be driven
by lust and therefore
innocent. I say innocent
because how else to explain
Alexandria. Raised out of a bay's polluted waters
the world's richest underwater dig
turned up sphinxes and pharos. Dawn:
a hunk of dark stone being hauled from the water.
They say it took twenty such blocks
to build the first lighthouse in history.
The Great Pyramid at Giza, the Mausoleum at Halicarnassus—
these too were wonders of the ancient world.
And the relentless torso—twelve tons of goddess
lifted on her back out of a watery bed.
At the sight of her breasts the filthy sky seemed to brighten.
Why am I looking into the pool of her navel?
Because here at the quay I'm trying to remember
a stormy night in 1374. A beacon
still guided incoming vessels
but a year later an earthquake reduced it to legend.
Sometimes I see a child staring out of that lighthouse window.
She's frightened, for all I know she was drugged
and sold for a piece of silver. For all I know
she leaped forward in time, was the Egyptian woman
who strapped a camera on her back and walked underwater.
I can see her dark head, sleek as a seal's
moving among the fishes, I mean,

among the fishes and sphinxes. This too
comes back to me now: how raptly I listened
to Mrs. Ward, my seventh-grade teacher.
Her field of passion was a watery ruin.
For weeks she held us captive
telling of pharos and rumours of pharos:
for centuries people guessed pieces lay in the harbour.
Flinging chalk at our heads, she told how
a windlass hoisted fuel to the parapet
where a fire burned continuously. Did I say
*windlass*, did I say *parapet*? She said,
*Take care of your words, if they taste of salt crystal*
*they will crack a stone.*

Travelling the Floodwaters

## Grocery List

I don't want you meandering in the aisles.
You're not on a luxury cruise.
I know you, how you loiter

in the meat with finely dressed
women, gathering tips
on rare cuts and choice prices.

Bleach as you can see
is foremost on my mind.
The wonders of bleach fill my thoughts

like an invisible stain.
A thimbleful is all I'd need to disinfect
the words I've poured like germs

over this crisp white page.
The items which follow should reveal
how I package my dreams:

oysters crammed into rectangular
tins. Head on the pillow, I settle
like a cornflake, years past expiry date,

stale and boxed in. But you'll miss all this.
I've always said you read too quickly.
Such subtlety will fly

over your head like the sound
of a cash register. When I tell you
I want the cheese sliced,

the bread soft, and the avocados ripe,
what I mean is, it's time we developed
new eating habits, what I mean is

we're ready for change. Am I being
too explicit, too painfully allegorical
when I tell you the cart you push past

the dried fruit is my heart and I want you to fill it?
When I write *salad makings*
am I being too obscure?

When I underline
*tomatoes* do you understand
how necessary they are? For colour, I mean,

although you have fallen for some salads,
good-looking and all green. (Think of it:
artichoke hearts bearing themselves

on lettuce leaves, proud without shame,
like women on centrefolds. To be
that camouflaged, to be so unseen!)

## Looking for a Man

The day the fair came to town
Heather and I leaned out an upstairs window
watching our father walk down the street

holding a strange lady by the hand.
That night the screams and banging
on the door woke us but this time

he could go to hell and back
before Mother'd let him in.
That's when Heather and I stole

down the stairs and saw his hand
break through the window.
We stood and shivered in the silence

that always follows broken glass.
In nightgowns and bare feet
we crept outside and in the dark

followed drops of blood along the sidewalk.
Hugging an empty bottle
and curled upon a neighbour's lawn,

we found him crying. I'm going
to the fair tonight. I'm looking for a man
who doesn't bend and doesn't bleed.

Heather's crawling around the bars tonight.
She's looking for a man
whose hands are full of scars.

## Party Wounds

This morning I examine them—
the abrasion running down my back
like a strip of hot tape, the twisted ankle, swollen jaw.
The whiskey that slid down my throat like warm honey.
Struck by my own despair, I left the fireflies,
wine-crazed wasps, and flailing night bodies.
These are the wounds I gathered up in my arms
as though they were a bouquet of long-stemmed daisies.
Combined they developed monstrous proportions.
They became huge as the rock I pushed over the cliff.
These are the wounds I stuffed in a sack
and flung over my shoulder, stumbling
through the night as though it were
an uphill obstacle course.

# On Closer Inspection

1

Every morning you appear at my bedside,
a shadow spinning tales out of the night before.

I recognize you even at a distance
for you always come
a bucket full of coal
swinging loosely at your side.

On closer inspection
I see your pores are filled with soot
and unlike anyone I've known
a streak of platinum
runs through your hair
like an open flame.

*Some men*, you say, *are destined for the fire.*


2

Our life together
is a simple arrangement.
You turn me in your unsteady hand,
a nervous jeweller
examining his first black diamond.

And I, under such scrutiny,
ridicule anything that comes to mind.

3

Standing on my tombstone
you will declare you always loved me.
But your words will be muffled
as though spoken
from behind a closed damper.

I can imagine you stamping your foot,
obliterating my epitaph and swearing,

*I wore this woman like an extra coat of skin*
*for the same reasons*
*a coal man would wear satin gloves.*

*Because it was extravagant, absurd.*

## What Men Are Fond Of

Men are fond of lemon crepes with the high meringue topping.

Men are especially fond people.
And proud too.

Of their dexterity and precision when measuring the flour,
of their stamina when beating the batter,
especially proud of their perseverance
when treating the pan.

Men are not limited in their tastes.
They are interested in a variety of ways to top their crepes.
For instance, maple syrup and blueberries.

In general
men are not as fond of cream
as women are. For men, cream is a luxury,
an extra, something women imply they've forgotten
in order to criticize their overall
culinary performance.

But men
being basically generous and fond people
do not abandon their art
despite such intimations.

And women notice and appreciate
men who prepare their crepes slowly.

On the whole
women are fond of men,
especially of men who demonstrate
a certain mastery in the kitchen.

Melancholy Ain't No Baby

## Mad Enough

I am mad enough to drink
your last bottle of homemade beer,
mad enough to drink myself
into a halfhearted fury. See
what a feeble course my revenge takes.

I have eaten twenty-three spears
of asparagus smothered in butter and salt.
They tasted good but not good enough.

Five pink tulips
stand like candles on the kitchen table.
The evening sun through the skylight
shines on the mahogany surface.
The table has been rubbed with lemon oil
and tulip leaves drip round the vase
like wax. I am mad enough
to fling these flowers across the room.

To write you out of this poem.
But I want you here
where I can see you.

## The Drums in Our House

The drums in our house roll when things get hot.
A great seething beat often shakes this wooden shack.

There is a lot to get hot about with us three
living as we do all winter long in these small cedar rooms.

The drums rumble through the ceilings, the tongue-
and-groove floors, they rumble up and down the chimney,

brick crumbles, we lose our balance, knock down lamps.
This is how it works: I complain there is not enough

love for me in these hot cramped rooms. He gets mad,
says I'd invent trouble in an empty house. We go to bed

in the afternoon and the drums don't roll so much
for the next few days. Then our daughter gets sick,

small as she is and the drums start up again, slow at first.
I think to myself, she has caught from me a disease

of the soul, and the drums gain momentum,
call in the cymbals, and really go to it.

# Fishbowl

What I want is to lie with you beside the fishbowl.

To have an absolute day of it.

Watching the fish
slip like gold leaves
round the inside of the bowl.

What I want is for all the bad luck
in the house to be absorbed by them
like the Chinese folktale says it will.

For their magic fins to swim alongside you everywhere.

Before you rise from bed
let me warn you:
there are glass bowls
in every room of the house.

Even in the attic
you will find their exquisite bodies
swimming madly round and round

knowing as they do
how suddenly glass can shatter.

## Summer Dreamed

A lost dream of mirrors
from which she awoke in fragments.
In June I lit up like a glowworm

just in time to dream myself
into Summer's size 7 dresses,
try on her new straw hat.

By July I was well-settled in the kitchen
where the dream opened wide as the screen door
and fell onto my lap.

Out by the woodpile
I held the hard body of a man so close
the dream broke into rivers and spread out in all directions.

Summer dreamed mosquitoes, dry wells, and forest fires.
I didn't blame her.
I dreamed these things too.

One night the dream slipped
through a hole in the blackberry patch.
A small girl swung through and cleared the sky.

Through August the child appeared:
at right angles to the dream,
eating an apple, wading in the sea.

As long as I could I dreamed cat dreams
in the tall yellow grass.
At times I couldn't get near

to where Summer was dreaming
her black jewels and tent of love.
Then suddenly, rocking on the porch and listening

to the frogs play the night like a piccolo,
I'd dream myself so close to Summer
I could taste the honey of her on my tongue.

# Longings
*—for Liam*


I was longing with a giant's thirst.
I was peekaboo partner pulling strings through the earth.

Struck with longing at fifteen-minute intervals
like the clock on the mantel.

Bottlenecked up to here one July morning
watching the sun rise with a holler.

I was mother again and the soles of my feet cool on the porch.
I was shout, laughter, champagne pop.

Swaddled in grape leaves by the little girl next door.
I was the smell of summer baby.

Slept nobly on my left side, sore and bruised
but never gave up my position.

I was an astonished face, a streetlamp beaming,
pavement shimmering after rain.

I was the French boy's dark eyes awash in the opera house.
I was voice shining.

Smitten and not new to it.
My hands bursting with your plump thighs.

## Short History

It was curiosity not love that caused my mother
to pick me from her garden. She said it was
my leaves — the way they seemed to recoil
when her foot came too near —
that first caught her eye.

She put me in a slender vase on her bedroom sill,
added vitamins and minerals to my water.
Small arms and legs developed from my stem.
Where a flower should have sprouted
I blossomed a head.

My mother claimed me as one of her own.
I was wrapped in a blanket, fed warm milk,
rocked in my sister's toy cradle.

Under this attention I grew hair, lungs, even a heart.
Everything needed to pass for human.

But my vegetable nature never left.
My teachers complained it was unnatural
to paint flowers with faces, draw families of weeds
(mother, father, children, and dog). And the stories
I wrote, the main character, always a scandalous piece of fruit.

I was reprimanded too for praying to the wrong God:
a giant shrub in the sky.

At sixteen everything I wore, from socks to nail polish,
a deep shade of forest. The walls of my bedroom

I painted the colour of spring grass.
My bicycle: gleaming emerald.

I became a strict carnivore.
At twenty would eat nothing that grew green from the earth.

At twenty-five was convinced I was suffering,
absorbing too little carbon dioxide, too much water.
The liquid around my brain
causing hallucinations.

A year later I climbed a wild apple tree,
stayed up there for six months
swallowing pills that smelled of chlorophyll.

You will need this short history.
It will help you explain to our children
why their mother left home
without kissing them good-bye.

# The Way to Eat Grass

The way to eat grass
as though it were soul-satisfying
and you believed in a soul:
hooves entrenched in mud,
many teeth chewing.

. . .

I have been warned that the road
to salvation is promising
as the sonorous moo in the distance.

. . .

In the forest
wild cows mingling with a version of deer,
following their trail.

. . .

Before the trails became paths.
Before the paths became dirt roads.
Before the men on the east side of the river
pulled the shades over their eyes
and took to the highway driving like demons.

. . .

I was found imitating the soft-shoe lowing of angels
one afternoon late in July.
I became holy
as the cry of a newborn calf.

. . .

What of the women's discretion?
How they pretend not to notice
the milk gone sour on their doorsteps,
the absence of bulls in the pen,
the nightly stampede across the horizon?

. . .

A symptom of my condition:
this tendency to seek out water,
to hover around the huge brown
of the cow's eye blinking.

. . .

In a dream I was more songful
than a songbird's song, a village schoolteacher
instructing small children on the unique
digestive tract of a cow.

. . .

When one of the herd is impatient
the rest become aware of their pointless existence.
Their protest of mooed obscenities is ignored
for it lacks imagination and rage.

. . .

I too would like to have been born
with a gazelle's grace
and friends beyond the fence.

. . .

I have heard mystics speak reverently
of a place where clover does not cover the pasture
only to find itself passed from stomach to stomach.

. . .

They say all it took was a gentle breeze.
Now the women of the west
no longer bicker with the women of the east.
Now they smile, even among themselves.

. . .

I was born with vague intimations
and a dread of rampageous men.
With a conviction
that a mighty carnivore roams in heaven.

. . .

What will get me in the end
is this need to graze solitaire,
to ruminate and defend my isolation.
This mad urge to graze graze graze.

The Mad and Beautiful Mothers

## As Sure as They Were Born

I open the kitchen door and walk in.
My sisters are sitting at the table
drinking tea, eating those small Scottish
pancakes we liked so much with plum jam.
My mother holds a cigarette under the table,
exhales smoke discreetly out the corner of her mouth.

They all stop talking.

My sisters' china cups
clatter into saucers as sure as they were born.
Their brows knit beneath long straight bangs,
my mother guards her cigarette so well
not one of them suspects:
after all these years
she hasn't quit.

I sit in the chair nearest the oil stove.
I am wearing a skirt and jacket
made out of the green curtains
that once hung in every room of this house.

My sisters are outraged.

That I have grown up.
Walk about town in all kinds of weather,
our well-kept family secrets draped over my body.

*I suppose you're happy now*, my mother says,
forgetting herself, pointing with the cigarette
at the bare window above the sink.
*Now anyone can see in.*

# The Mad and Beautiful Mothers

We are the children of the fifties
with the mad and beautiful mothers.
In the forties they went to movies in toeless
high heels, smoked cigarettes, and dreamed
of Leslie Howard, their madness
occurring some time later.

Perhaps it struck the night we were born
or that day at the park, swinging from our knees
we slipped from the bars. After that,
clotheslines collapsed in every backyard,
and children fell through the air
like bombs in September.

We left for school and they barricaded the doors
with living room furniture. Later,
we climbed in through basement windows,
twisted and jived to rock 'n' roll
while upstairs our mothers bent over sinks,
unable to wash their hair.

We hid our mothers from our friends,
our friends from our mothers. Thunder
and lightning and some disappeared into closets
or hospitals from which they never emerged.
Perhaps madness first struck on that flight
from Amsterdam, London, Glasgow, the cabin
hot and crowded, and rain seeping in.

We learned to shift our lives
around and through them where they sat
at the dining room table staring through doors
in the wallpaper for days at a time.
We are the children who survived the fifties
and their mothers, even their conversations with God.

It has taken us years to forgive them
their madness, though they loved us despite it.
Years to go back to the muggy afternoons
the whole world reeked
of spice and sweat and vinegar.

It is late August and our mothers are in the kitchen
pickling beets and cucumbers.
Like fiends they are pickling
silver-skinned onions
and anything else
that gets in their way.

## Summer Vacation

Those August nightmares, sailing through them.

The blue Pontiac, shiny as a missile, the journey up and down
the island each summer, one week by the sea,
bivouacked in a cottage.
The awful coming and going, your shell-shocked father
ten years home from the war.

Your mother sat in the backseat, a grim saint,
between you and your sister. Never contradicted him,
never told him to goddamn slow down.

He'd speed lethally past every vehicle, screaming *road hog*
out the window at stunned vacationers.

Your father played chicken, doubled-dared the car
streaking head-on toward you. He'd pull back
into your lane with nothing but your lives.

For three hundred kilometres of mined highway
you and your sister kept diving to the floor
though your bodies never did burst from their skins.

# Edinburgh Rock

In jaunty pedal pushers I walked beside my grandmother
while she pushed the buggy containing
whichever of my cousins
was the baby at the time.
No matter which route we took
through the streets of Greenock,
eventually we'd pass the orphanage.
The place, she never failed to explain,
where bad children went. Plucked,
it seemed, from their mothers' loving arms.
A proliferation of buttercups and fear filled that summer.
Each evening I stole rock candy
from the tin beside my grandmother's bed
and each morning I walked past
that stark prison. I remember
her scrubwoman's hands,
the pride she took in her jet black hair
years after her friends had gone bald or grey.
The sound of the buggy's wheels
slowing, coming to a stubborn halt,
my grandmother reminding me
that hundreds of them, just about my age,
slept in tiny cells without windows.
Thieving hands shoved into pedal-pusher pockets,
I heard with sinking heart
how in ice-cold water
they washed their own clothes.

# Weird Genes

Aunt Rebecca's daughters, eight years apart,
all walked in their sleep like their father.
She said my oldest cousin began
her journey into the dark at three years old.
Ran the bath full of cold water, took off
her nightgown, returned naked to bed.
The next one with wild red hair was regular as clockwork.
A winter night when she opened all the windows,
the front and back doors, set the table
with her mother's best china. At four
the youngest girl sat at the edge of her bed
and expertly laced up her skates though
my aunt said she couldn't do this for herself
at the rink on Saturday afternoons.
She stumbled through the house, blades cutting into
hardwood floors, dreaming ice, dreaming popcorn, dreaming
figure eights. Once my aunt woke to my uncle
standing on a chair, flashlight in hand,
peering out a window boarded up years before.
She confessed to my mother it drove her mad.
Years of sticking bone-handled knives
between the jamb and their bedroom doors
to keep them in. A lifetime of waking up
to furniture rearranged, lamp shades in the garden,
the fridge emptied, false teeth on the back porch.
Said it was a good thing her husband's brothers never married,
a blessing their weird genes were contained
on a small sheep farm in northern Wales.
A chill going up her spine Aunt Rebecca imagines
those four bachelors wandering the mountains
of Snowdonia: wide-eyed, in nightcaps,
bereft of their musical tongues.

# Sculpture

All the ten-year-old girls in the world are washing their hair
they are sudsing it up with soap that smells of green apples
they are kneeling in rivers and bathtubs and glacial pools
they are washing their blond or black or auburn hair sculpting

the stuff into spikes and curls they are laughing and calling
their mothers from gardens or books or the youngest child
helmets and crowns whip like cream on top of their heads
all over the world mothers are seeing their daughters

as never before perhaps it's the last time these girls will be
perfect as long-stemmed lilies all arms and legs and beautiful
eyes the mothers are standing in doorways or crouching on
sandbanks all over the world the sun drops behind mountains

or violet clouds and the mothers turn back to their other
concerns wondering about these girls who rinse their hair not
once but twice who step from the water shaking their heads and
smelling of apples where in the world will they go from here.

## Daylight Savings

I will remember how you sang yourself to sleep
the night half the world changed their clocks forward,
an orange dump truck in one hand,
a red bulldozer in the other.

I will remember your singing
and the prospect of that extra hour of light.
How I stood outside your bedroom door
to hear your words more clearly,
the dump truck and bulldozer
assuming personalities
distinct as sisters, two years apart.

How I went to bed to read and set the clock,
but how, before turning out the light,
I returned to kiss you one more time,
and found you sleeping, the dump truck
on the pillow, pressed against your cheek.

And I will remember the sudden affection
I felt for those Tinkertoys
because they were
small and battered
and because
you sang to them.

## At the Cabin in August

He was small when he first spoke of it,
that *Bleak Heaven*. Small where he slept

beyond the staircase immaculate as a word
stripped of meaning. Those mornings

he walked into the kitchen in yellow pyjamas,
a fat novel under his arm. After dinner

we sat at the table, night falling like blue rain
through the skylight. *And who wrote this book,*

*this Bleak Heaven? we asked, did you?*
We lay in bed a long time, marvelling.

That he, so small and with damp curls,
should invent with such tenderness.

*Bleak Heaven*: a masterpiece
so pure it tore all night at our hearts.

# Indian Summer

You're having a nervous breakdown
but there's no joy in it, no sense of floodgates
opening. Your husband makes you laugh;
you're so absurd lying in a heap
on a Saturday morning. Your children
walk through your dark room: *Not again, not
again, can we go to the store to buy candy?*

At noon you force yourself out of bed,
dress in your cocktail clothes. Nevertheless
you are drawn into corners, dumbstruck.
Even as you stand there dust settles on the ledges.

Your friend drops by, nods wisely.
She'd seen it coming. Not even poetry
can hold back the flu or a nervous breakdown.

You know the end of October is a bad time for it,
seventy degrees in the shade, the light all wrong,
your shadow too. Last night
it stretched out so far it turned the corner and strode off.

Like the last plum of summer you fall and fall.
As you descend
golden skins
peel from your body
and you remember your childhood
as a long hallway of light, the smell of new dolls,
their yellow hair.

## National Enquirer: Baby Obsession

There's the fetus ghost that torments
its eighty-three-year-old mother, furious
at being aborted, or the baby
born with three heads, each fluent
in a different French dialect.
The one born with a tail, complete

with an extra pea-sized brain.
But the story I like best is
"The Russian Water Babies."
How they've been seeded like plants
off the shore of Vladivostok.
Like fat red tomatoes

they are ripening right now.
Soon, they're going to rise up,
identical birthmarks, hammer
and sickle, stamped on their foreheads.
Stride across the Pacific, undaunted
and undetected by the Mounted Police

or CIA. I like to think of them
marching across the ocean floor
in diapers and bonnets, strips of kelp
caught round their necks, trailing behind
like shiny green ribbons.
Unstoppable

as Leinengen's ants or Christ's
Second Coming, this army
of infants will cut their first teeth

on fishermen's nets. Through fathoms
of darkness, schools of killer whales, cooing,
gurgling, an acre of bubbles rising to the surface.

I want to be on the beach
when they step from the water,
wave upon wave, blinking in new light.
Already I can hear their little tin trumpets.
And look! Where the mountains tremble, the horizon
shimmers — ten thousand rattles flashing in the sun.

# Extremities of Madness and Love

Last night in bed we were talking,
not able to sleep because every ninety seconds or so
a voice called, *Glenda I love you*, at first
we thought it funny that someone should stand
on the sidewalk of a perfectly residential street
and howl like a Himalayan mountain dog,
as though Glenda could hear him,
whoever, wherever she was,
then after a bit we just lay there
listening, the entire neighbourhood stopped
arguing or turning pages or making love, even
the children settled into their restless sleep
waiting for the next call to split the night
while whoever he was sucked in his breath
and ninety seconds later hurled *Glenda*
*I love you* back into the dark, finally I said,
*I can't stand this, that maniac's going to wake*
*the kids, I'm going to give him*
*hell or call the police, who does he think he is*
*standing practically outside our window*
*screaming like an idiot* but you held
my arm, whispered, *No*
*don't stop him*, in the half-light
your eyes almost pleading, I'd forgotten
how deeply you respect another man's pain,
I'd forgotten this sad broken song
had once been our own.

## Winsome

Something tells me there's a horse in this neighbourhood
and it's not the smell of lilac

though it does make the world taste much sweeter.
You travel down its sunny side in a luxury coach,

while somewhere in this neighbourhood
a horse wants out. I've heard that neigh before:
winsome, brokenhearted.

I could say

I miss you like a horse would miss
the taste of summer hay but.
Where would that leave me?
Pawing the ground?

I watched TV late and alone.
White light flooding the living room
with bad news, ominous news.
The oceans have had it.
The forests / air / rivers /
ozone layer too.

You lean forward in a reclining seat
but who's that beside you?
The woman laughing at all your jokes.
And love? On top of her head,
a little coconut tree.

Out of time and out of turn, my best companion
just when the day was beginning
to smell so sweet.

Those Were the Mermaid Days

## 3.59

The minute I was born
Roger Bannister ran the miracle mile.

My mother tells me this all these years later.

How the priest breezed in to congratulate her,
glibly announce that she and Roger
had both come through.

She cursed that priest out of the room, screaming
it *was* a miracle, a bloody miracle
she survived at all —
ankles strapped down in stirrups,
doped like an animal.

But I am not interested
in early forms of female torture,
ask why she's never told me before
that I was swimming into the world
against gravity and all good sense
while somewhere a man tore
round a track defying the limits
of human performance.

How to explain the kinship, the igniting of my birth?

Despite my mother's bruised ankles and slurred speech
it seems to me now
a sweet and rare miracle.

This stranger and I,
like two separate thoughts,
blazing through the barriers of an inscrutable brain.

## Something Crazy

Eighteen, with a one-way
ticket, that time you were leaving
him for good. At the airport
he snatched me from my stroller,
dove into a waiting taxi.
They say you raved for three
mad weeks while in some secret
room of the city I was a little bomb,
ticking. He finally phoned; the police
chief warned you not to rush
at him when he came to the station:
*He might do something crazy*
*with the kid.* How blue
was the prairie sky that morning
we all converged in the back
parking lot? Was I hungry,
did I coo or cry to see
the men in dark uniforms
closing in, curious as children
surrounding a recess scuffle?
My aunt says you looked beautiful
in a sleeveless dress and green
sandals, that you waved
and smiled so sweetly
anyone would have sworn
it was love. For a moment
we might have been any family.
The tall father holding out
the baby, the young mother
reaching up with a sigh.

# Sepia Folk

Cinnamon cloves boiled in an open pot.
For years morning light stung
my eyes when I stepped out for school.
A jungle of cactus and ferns, that basement
apartment was also a zoo. Every stray
within miles rubbed its mangy
path to our welcome mat.
There was the hamster that slept
in my hair, the goldfish on the kitchen
table — swimming glass centrepiece.
The crow our cat pulled down from the cherry tree.
Soon it perched on my shoulder
while my mother dropped kernels
of wet bread into its beak. For years
she spent her days sifting through the junk
of secondhand stores. She'd buy
old photographs though not like other people
for their ornate frames. She adopted
these sepia folk, gave them
biblical names like Zerubbabel
and Tirzah. The dead
hung on our walls, the glass
they stared through fogging over
with cinnamon steam. They were
my great-uncles, second cousins,
the Norwegian grandparents I never knew.
I believed my mother when she told me
these cast-off relatives had been abandoned
by their descendants. How lucky,
I thought, how good she'd found them.

# The Green Girl
*— for Danika*


The green girl lives behind the wall,
all the children say so.
The small ones won't go down there

alone. That winter morning
she slouched against the water
fountain while we kicked

and pinched and shrieked, *Are you alive?*
How we howled up the basement
stairs, dragged our chalk-smudged

teacher from the classroom —
vanished, she was gone!
In time even we remember

only vaguely how she sagged
and hung her head. Before we knew
the stuff of sadness she was

punched with grief, wan
as straw. Each spring we turn
the rope at recess, jump and skip

a dead girl's chant. In groups
of three we press our ears
against the tiles. Some hear

laughter, others breathing;
I hear nothing then her hand
slips out. One by one

and thin as wafers we pass
from the tumult of our bodies
to the other side.

## Gurkha: The Word We Loved

He shut the curtains, opened his father's bottom drawer.
We were nine, school almost out, the days growing long
as the final hours of the Second World War.
He walked toward me balancing a leather scabbard
in his open palms. Gripped the ornate handle,

slowly pulled out the short, curled blade. *Every man
in Nepal wears one, a kukri*, the boy said, wishing
he wore one too. We stood facing each other
in the dead part of the day, looking down
at the eloquent steel weapon and I guess

I was impressed with the Gurkha's gift to his father.
After that, whenever his parents were out we'd steal up
to their bedroom, take turns holding the knife,
the boy telling stories his father had told him.
How the Gurkhas fought with the British;

silent as cats they'd creep along the desert
feeling for the laces of a soldier's boots.
Their fingers were eyes in the dark
that could see the difference.
Depending on how you'd tied your bows

they'd slit your throat or whisper *pssst Johnny*,
before slipping back into the hills. Or
they'd murder every second German in his sleep.
*To undermine morale*, the boy would say,
wishing he'd thought of that. But it was

the word, not the knife, we loved most.
Passed it from tongue to tongue, repeating
its rich, guttural sound. *Gurkha*,
I'd say, scalp tingling, while outside
the other kids played cowboys and Indians

into the ordinary evening. *Gurkha*, the boy'd say,
thinking: dark-skinned angel, magician of death.
Wishing he could drop through the tent
of history, land in the enemy camp
on panther paws.

## Elopement

Before breakfast I threw my wedding
clothes out the bathroom
window, God bless that spring
and all who lived through it.
My blouse and stockings
were soaked with dew.
We might have gone
to the dentist, that morning
we might have stomped through the cow pasture.
Rode bicycles into the city.
Took vows in a small blue room
without windows or bridesmaids.
It's been years since my father said nothing
then slammed the kitchen door.
In the rose garden my mother's face
was a blank sundial at noon.
I remember our bodies —
lawless as weapons, flutes
always going up in flame.
After the ceremony we sat on a bluff
overlooking the ocean.
For hours not speaking.
Gulls swung through the air.
Among the raspberry canes
my father rose like a white pillar,
fists at his sides. Over the cliff
we dangled boots caked in yesterday's
mud and then across
the Juan de Fuca Strait
lights went on
all over America.

## After Supper the Parents Look Up

The neighbourhood children climb the wall
of cedar hedge, thirteen
swarm the branches,
heads emerging and circled in light.

At the top, three girls sit apart on a leafy scaffold.
Like chimps, they pick twigs and bugs
from each other's sweaters and hair.

A small one glances down
at us, openmouthed spectators.
Arms folded, we are weighty as judges
demanding an explanation. Are these the children
who only an hour ago fought over mitt and bat?

A boy calls, *I am coming,*
and butts through the snarled limbs.
A hand reaches down, pulls him up by invisible thread.

One is puppet, the other puppeteer.
Or is this a kind of birth?

The children travelling up
the cedar trunks,
soft skulls
pushing into the sky.

# Beginning of Fear

Lately you are fascinated with Indians.
We return home with library books
on the Iroquois, Algonquin, Apache.
When we get to the Hopi
it's like stumbling
upon an oasis in the desert
of war. No time or inclination
to paint their faces, too busy planting corn.
In bed I read and reread this gentle tribe.
Beside me you lie on your back,
mind fixed on the Creek—
the chief who danced outside
his thatched hut loudly mustering
his braves. They'd steal to the next village,
torch the walls of sleeping neighbours,
crouch behind trees and shoot their fleeing enemies.
You stare at the ceiling, hands tucked
behind your head and I want to say
you are my son, I would protect you, pull you
into my adobe house and raise
the ladder but already you are running
into the night, the pointless
arrow entering your breast.

# Following the Garbage Truck

Once I fell in love with the garbage-
men, from a distance we grew
acquainted like crocuses in grass.
My son was two and when their truck
whined and snorted three blocks away,
he'd holler and we'd run from the house,
follow that belching dragon
through tunnels of flowering trees,
the garbagemen gripping its side
and grand as a Chinese New Year.
That spring my marriage
was an empty bottle
clattering over the brink.
But the men in thick gloves
returned every week
and for the price of our lives
carried away the sad junk of ours.
They rode high on the truck,
its huge metal belly
burping tins and broken glass.
I remember them leaning like acrobats
into the perfumed air, thinking,
nothing could save me
from the wreck of that winter,
holding onto my son's hand
as he gambolled in the stink
and wake of bliss.

# Dream of the Orphanage

My sister and I fly to Romania.
We've heard about the babies banging their heads
against metal bars. It seems we are their mothers,
have come to bundle them home.

My sister bends over the shrivelled body
of a two-year-old boy. Her arms
are a cedar basket lifting him close to her heart.

I search the cupboards for what I can find
in this dark country, a mop, pail, box of soap flakes.
I begin to scour the stone walls.

My sister rushes past on her way to the airport.
Carrying a dark-haired child, she promises
to send me bleach, rubber gloves.

The plane dissolves into a purple sky,
becomes the scrub brush I hold in my hand.

At the dream's end I am kneeling in milky suds
and the babies of Romania are rocking themselves
in a thousand cribs. A forty-watt bulb
shines on the rows of orphans: it is
their unlucky star.

# Saturday Night Dance at the Boy Scout Hall

Fifteen years of yanking
each other this way and that.
This dance cannot work with two
wanting to lead, neither knowing
the steps. As a boy
you came up for air, heard your father
say to the lifeguard
the pool was half-decent.
The glorious indifference of that word.
You used it to describe whatever you could:
a yo-yo, your sister's beehive, later,
the LSD bought from a friend.
Tonight we jerk around this room
avoiding the tried-and-true couples
who glide to sublime blue music.
Like children, we stumble
and count, *onetwothree*
*onetwothree*, when suddenly
we've got it, this waltz is half-decent!
Surrounded by wilderness murals
we cling to each other
looking down at our amazed feet.
And when we look up —
the bear has a fish in its paw,
the owl and the deer are watching.

## Blue Salt and Silence

The way I walked with you, Father, the last days of your life.
Helpless, begging you to live. *You'll be happy,*

I said. *You could travel, paint, sculpt with the clay*
*we dig from the cliffs near my house.* Arm in arm

we walked, warm gusts blowing in from the ocean —
bright red kites! At every bench you stopped to rest.

I could not reclaim your body or years, the moon
which rolled like a beach ball over water. You wept

in my arms like a child after a day of learning to walk.
Of falling and falling and sand in the eyes. Father,

the way your breath caught in your lungs.
In that blue salt and silence: a bird strangled in cloud.

## Foxes Also, Lying in Wait

Your death has rolled over us like a boulder.
It has careened down the alley where once we stood laughing
in yellow dresses. We take our grief into closets

so our children will not hear it. We continue
to shop for rice and oranges as though you were reading
a newspaper on the blue floral couch, and we

could walk up the hill to your house, kiss your cheek.
Our husbands cook the next meal with the last
tomatoes from your greenhouse. It is too early

to visit your gravesite by the sea. You have gone first,
just as when we were small you led the way, up the stairs
to our attic rooms. You switched on the lights —

tarantulas scattered, foxes also, lying in wait.
We dream you are on the other side, disappointed.
You thought death would be better than it is.

You cannot watch us, even from a distance.
You strain to see your grandchildren ride bicycles
up and down a sidewalk of fog. In these dreams

there is no end to the weeping. It rained
the day of your funeral, for weeks after your death.
Oak leaves carpeted your terraced gardens. Ankle-deep,
we raked and raked. At dusk, soggy piles dotted the lawns.
On the phone our mother's voice is hunchbacked, yes, its soul
stolen. We hold our children, nightly make love to our husbands.

We want to forget sometimes that our legs have collapsed
like wooden pins, that you were the first, the best
man in our lives and your death has rendered us useless.

## Bits of the Earth

In the eye of the hurricane pink frogs
ride from one continent
to another, a golden-
winged warbler is blown across
the Atlantic and two thousand bird lovers
invade a London cathedral to hear it sing.
It is happening all the time, bits of the earth
transported from here to there. You,
lifted from life, carried in a black car
to a seaside plot you did not want to enter.
And then there's the boy who ached
like a lover. Committed suicide,
leaving a note saying,
he just couldn't wait,
believed death
the ultimate adventure.
We stood on a wooden bridge
and the swans closed around us.
You told me then it was fear that kept you alive.
Father, I would have wished you
that boy's composure, the fanatic's calm.
To step with him into the cyclone's dead
centre as though it were a spaceship
and both of you bound
for a wiser world.

## Social Studies Report

I am thinking of the country tucked like a stitch
in the side of a continent, third largest
in South America but still
small. For weeks I lay on my stomach
poring through *National Geographics*,
collecting facts as though they were marbles:

the Incas, their temples of cut stone;
Lake Titicaca, four thousand metres above sea level;
the Oroya Railway, tracks built in heaven.

Others plucked Brazil from the map,
lured by the Amazon and Mardi Gras.
Or Argentina for its cattle and cowboys.
Ecuador exported bananas, Chile
dribbled down the coast like a snake
from its skin. What I didn't know
in fourth grade. I am thinking
of why in a classroom of forty-three
only I chose Peru. Its capital city,

pale green on my tongue — Lima — like the flat beans
that grew in the spare lot between tomatoes
and corn. Peru was the bent shape
I traced over and over at the kitchen table,
pressing down on its borders
with a 2B pencil. I dove
into it, head first,

a major project, my own
hydroelectric dam. I needed
statistics, graphs, a llama. On a rough
sheet of paper my father sketched one with coloured pencils.
Surrounded by the Andes that llama stood
on the highest peak, at the top of the world.

I learned nothing of politics. What *Encyclopedia Americana*
failed to mention. Concentrated instead
on Agriculture, Fishing, Gross National Product.
From the library I took out books
with black-and-white photographs,
smiling Indians in ponchos and wide-brimmed hats.

Even then I knew I'd never visit. Tourism
was not a subheading. What about my pocketful of marbles,
my teachers, the textbooks, what they didn't say?
Genocide in the jungle, peasants squashed
between ocean and mountain range,
junta and drug baron. Peru was

the rust earth the llama stood on, the tilt of its head.
I am thinking of my father's hand
shading in, quickly before dinner,
a pink and turquoise sky.

More Watery Still

# When the Body Speaks to the Heart It Says

I am a hunter-gatherer,
busy climbing the high ridge to watch where birds
will settle. I am flailing my arms,
picking huckleberries all day long.
I don't ask for much —
sex, a piece of cooked meat.
Waist-deep, I stop in salal, I am trying to be
ruffed as a grouse. On my knees
at the edge of the lake
I must fathom
how to pull fish from water.
I am animal, you can't blame me, this
is how I was made — hormones
and glands and ancient
predilection. See,
where I sleep by the fire —
my skull so vulnerable, my skin no protection at all.
The way I moan and curl
in on myself
I look like a newborn rat.
You may want love, beauty, the ineffable things
but I am not interested
in what you want.

## The Man on the Dust Jacket

The man on the dust jacket
wears a white shirt open at the collar,
is blond, and looks as though he might once
have been a tennis star, like my husband
might look in twenty years.
He's smiling but his eyes say,
I've lived long enough now
to know the nights are easy, it's the days
that are getting so hard.
This evening I read the book several times through
while my husband wonders aloud—
*is it possible*
*for a woman your age to fall in love*
*with a man on a dust jacket?*
And if I said yes
I would like to step into the stranger's table
of contents, his biographical note,
and wide smile? Climb the tree
of his body, lie down
in the leaves? Tonight
in the solid, dark house I stand on the landing
running a finger down the book's spine.
When do I begin to see past his face
to a room lit by kerosene lamps?
He's bent over an old kitchen table
writing a poem which begins in confusion
but ends with a man opening
a gate, a woman in white shorts
walking down to the grass
courts by the river.

# In the Ravine

Who could sleep?

Nights I woke to the torrent
that once roared through the valley.

In the city's memory
forests still flourish in swamps —
huge conifers and seed ferns.

We dropped into the ravine
and the world was pungent as yeast.

All week I spun, a compass berserk,
the needle searching for star
or good omen. Pressed my face
against a subway window
unable to navigate
the heart's circumference.

In October, light declines so we followed it
down: just us and the city's smallest
inhabitants. The children
flew along the gorge, bright pterodactyls.

Later, we climbed steps
pounded into rock while behind us
thunder lizards
rose from mud the velvet
colour of apricots.

I headed south into rush-hour traffic
and you drive north
to your wife and sons.

# First Love

He turns off the light and drags a kitchen chair
into the middle of the room. He sits, pulls me onto
his lap. I wrap my arms and legs around
all of him, hold his head close.
We stay that way a long time,
saying nothing.

In a week he will fly to England. It's the end
of August and for two hot days we shop
for things he will need to backpack through Europe.
He buys me a James Taylor record,
it's the first record I own.

The night before he leaves we go to a party.
I stand on the back porch. A huge willow tree
canopies the yard. From inside the house
I hear him say, *Where's she gone?*
Green light slides down the branches.

In September I return to school.
My friends treat me with a new kindness, I have
the status of a woman whose husband has gone to war.
For three months I write letters every night
after dinner, I sit cross-legged
on my bed listening to *Sweet Baby James*.

At the end of November I bundle the letters
in a box and bring them to his mother. She will
deliver them in two days when she meets him in Italy.
At the Rome airport, wouldn't you know it,
she loses that one suitcase.

He flies home for Christmas.
I walk into his bedroom and he's got his arms
around a woman who's weeping, stroking his cheek.
For a moment I can't decide
and then I recognize his mother's voice.

I can't move—
the sight of them embracing like lovers.
His mother looks over his shoulder, she stares
through me as though I'm a glass girl.

I sit in the kitchen and wait for him to remember
last summer. His youngest sister comes in and opens
the fridge door, she is looking for ice cream.
The lightbulb's broken and the room remains dark.

Then she is a blind animal moving toward the sound
of a heartbeat. Blond and marsupial,
she climbs the front of my body.
She sits on my lap and begins
to play with my hair.

# Pregnancy

It happens like this: you are a child yourself,
not sure of the details, you were drinking
milk with that boy in his mother's
kitchen, eating cold lasagna, earlier
you'd walked on the beach. Just
once, just like that, a slip
of the tongue? A visit to the doctor's
and you wait by the phone.
Her voice travels from Jupiter, hesitates —
*positive.* You tumble backwards,
the solar system blacks out.
You pretend as children do: *it isn't so,*
become inventive, dress in smocks,
and breeze past your friends.
They don't notice as you fill more
and more space. Alone in your bedroom
you unbutton your blouse, suck in
your breath, you stand before the mirror, see,
you are slim as a reed. And then
the butterfly wings, the kick below the rib cage.
In the bath your stomach shifts
like a landmass. You hate it hate it, rock
all night not sure who you wail for.
In time your body forgets
you, begins to speak another language.
In the middle of a sentence
it walks away from the boy
in your French class, his white sports car
already a loose speck in the distance.

# Among the Yellow Lilies

I was in the garden pulling morning
glory off the fence when she
dropped between my legs.
I hadn't felt a pang, not a flicker of pain.
Like a pearl she must have formed in secret.
All morning I'd been yanking
but when I reached behind the peony
she slid from my body.
Among the yellow lilies —
an Easter egg,
the only one my children hadn't found.
I took off my gloves
and held her in one hand,
she was that small. Unlike my others
this one was serene, translucent.
She had that fetal face
we recognize as alien or divine.
I lingered that day and all week
believing she would waken,
in time, she'd cry out.
The seasons came and went.
Though the storms of January slammed
the coast I stood beside the fence
holding to her with a love that darkened the world.
This spring, trumpet flowers
twine the stone figure I've become
and still her bluish lids
do not open.

# Geese and Girls

At the end of summer you are thirteen
and bored at the cabin, ask
to walk alone the three kilometres to Prior Lake.
Your body is restless
as though after years of sleep
it wants to step out, look around.
*No*, I say, thinking of trucks
parked in the woods, beer
tins strewn along the dirt road.
You plead: *Just as far*
*as the stream, then, the first bridge.*
This afternoon you and your cousins
swam in the lake. From the wharf
your father and I watched.
Geese slid through the water
while you floated on your back,
arms and legs sprawled over
an inner tube
and I thought of a bird
grown too big for its nest.
*A playpen*, you sneer, *I'll be twenty-one*
*and still living in a playpen.*
And if I said, OK, but carry this breadknife,
for protection take this small axe?
I know curiosity, how it riots
the blood, you want to bang on the door
of the world, enter. But I am
every mother whose child's been gutted,
thrown in some ditch. Weeping
you say it's my fierce
attitude you hate, O my girl,
I hate it too.

# The Dead Body of My Friend

I was given the dead body of my friend
but I did not dress her in white,
I did not dig a place in the forest
or throw hyacinths into her grave.
I am afraid to think of what I have done.
If you knew you would not eat beside me
on the terrace, you would not offer me
another tangerine. I should tell someone,
the police or my oldest sister. Listen:
I was given the arms and legs, the fine head
of my friend but I did not cover them
with pine needles. Once, I came upon
this friend washing her dog in the river.
When she led it onto the bank I saw
how old and blind the dog had become.
From a bridge above I watched her wind up
the path, encouraging each limping step.
I will go look for my friend.
I must tell her what I have done and not done.
There she is now guiding the animal
out of the water.

## Naked Women

On the phone my sister says, *Did I ever tell you*
*about that magazine of naked women, the one Hilary found*
*under the driver's seat of her father's Pontiac?*

Hilary's dad! Ludicrous
to imagine him driving to the lumberyard at 7 a.m.,
lunch bucket rubbing his thigh. Stopped at a red light
and flipping through the pages.

*They stood before full-length mirrors,*
my sister says, *I guess for a front and back view.*

I ask if the women wore anything, on their feet,
for instance, did they wear those fluffy
pink slippers, can she remember
high-heel sandals? And their hair —
was it backcombed, done in French rolls?

*For God's sake*, she says, *it was a long time ago,*

though I remember that Pontiac's horn, jumping
up and down in the backseat, Hilary's father
driving us to the peninsula where we stole
vegetables from the fields. On the way home
crunching small dirty carrots.

*Actually they were quite tasteful,*
my sister says, *today those photographs*
*might be considered art.*

After we hang up I can't let go of those women,
of wanting them to mean something else.
Who knows? Maybe they'd been working
in the garden all afternoon. I want the phone
to stop ringing, the baby to cease crying,

dirt under the fingernails. I want
those women to be somebody's mother
after she's peeled off her blouse and shorts
and turned unthinking toward the mirror.

Our own mother perhaps. On each page
her look of exhaustion before
stepping into the bath.

## Choosing a Picture to Live With

You can find my mother in the graveyard.
It is not death she is drawn to but the unruffled sky,
the place itself, so sure of its purpose.

She walks the labyrinth of paths
scattering long-stemmed carnations.
Among chestnut trees and marble tombstones
she is a tartan sail, her skirt flapping.

Growing up I rarely saw my mother outside
the dowdy clothes of household chores.
Once I writhed in my desk at school —
Visitors' Day and where was she?
I think I gasped aloud. A flash of lipstick,
black curls — a movie star who'd wandered into
the wrong set? Washed up against the world
map, my mother obliterated pale seas, pastel continents.

These days she's drawn to the cemetery.
Every bitter word tucked away, nothing left but love
abridged, composed on stone.

Again I twist and crane my neck, again
she stops to read some tragic dates, moves toward
but cannot reach, my father's grave.

On earth we have no choice but to bend to grief,
we must choose a picture we can live with.
If she comes this way I will tell my mother,
*I choose you in a red coat*
*walking through that classroom door.*

## Solitude

I sat at the white desk under the skylight
thinking of all you'd said. It was raining.
I opened my notebook and wrote a list of the things
I desired most in the world. I began with the broad strokes
of summer but the list went on and on. *Solitude*
hung nearby, she was a framed print of a girl deep in thought.
It was November, that time of year when we all go searching.
For a river, perhaps, where ancient fig trees
grow along the banks. *Solitude's*
chin pressed into her palm, she wept but there were no tears.
A boy marked like a tropical fish appeared above my head.
On the other side of the skylight his face slipped
through the dark. Sorrow broke, wave upon wave.
Night was black as leather and smelled of pumpkins.
The boy with avocado skin swam out of my vision.
I closed my notebook and turned off the lamp.
Things became watery and then
more watery still.

# What I Remember from
# My Time on Earth

# The Origins of the Kiss

I wish to speak of origins:
the snail's caress, its antennae and the roots
growing deep in the earth.
I wish to speak of the duck's bill,
guillemots nibbling each other's feet,
the pose of any feathered thing.
I have traced the kiss to Semitic antiquity,
beyond Africa and its asexual wild grasses.
Homer scarcely knew it, the Greek poets seldom mentioned
the kiss though it took the rest of Europe
by surprise. In Lapland
the kiss was the centre of gravity,
you planted it just below the navel where a pool
of sex-water lay. In Celtic tongues
there was no word for it and so I sat alone
in a farmhouse trying to invent
a name. The Welsh kissed
only on special occasions, at a game
called *carousel*. Whenever there is rope-playing
there is also moonlight, and then one
came to me, shaped like a beet or pear.
Throughout East Asia the kiss was unknown,
in Japanese literature pleasure was intense.
The kiss has always been alive
in the ravings of schizophrenics, reveries
of satyrs — a theta wave in the alchemist's brain.
During lovemaking the Tamils licked each other's eyelids.
I wish to speak of such tenderness, the wisdom
inherent in voluptuous acts.
In the light of Palestine the kiss grew
in the incandescent spaces between olives trees.
Among early Christians: of sacramental significance —

kiss the relic of a saint, foot of the pope.
In Rome the kiss was a sign of reverence
and so the erotic possibilities did not become
flesh. Was it
the terrible kiss of God
that caused the virgins of central Russia to lose
consciousness and turn into
dock leaves? In Borneo
nose-pressing was the kiss of welcome and of mourning.
Arabian deities were easily uncaged
when about to receive kisses. Powerful
the impulse and yet the Chinese thought it cannibalistic.
Among the hill tribes of India:
olfactory, nose to cheek, *Smell me*, they said.
Mothers of the Niger coast rubbed their babies with their lips,
lovers did not. And the great unlit kiss
that feeds on mud at the bottom of the lake!
I wish to speak of the mammal's bite
and the hunger inside me, for every human infant.
Watch them. Their small fists
bringing each detail up to their mouths.

# The Dress

I worked in a stenographer's pool,
seven hours bent over a typewriter.

Mindless work but I liked that about it.

I bought the dress on a fifteen-minute coffee break.
Plenty of room to grow inside its full skirt.

It was 1977. I was hungry all the time.

The dress was white cotton.
It had spaghetti straps and fell just short of the ankles.

There was an economist
who liked to talk about poetry.

The other secretaries wondered but said nothing.

My mother left boxes
of baby clothes on the back doorstep.

Even the economist couldn't tell until that last month.

*It suits you*, he said, but I told him
I wanted to be myself a while longer.

My daughter is too much like me.
She does not give her love to what lies ahead.

If I saved things I would have saved her the dress.

But then I didn't know, I just didn't know.

# Rifle Range

We live in the forest and fir trees surround us like candles,
their tips graze the summer sky.
On a rock overlooking the valley
I push my daughter on a rope
so long and thick
she could be dangling
from a piece of thread tied to God's finger.
All morning the branch creaks like a sorrowing bone.
Afternoons it's three kilometres of gravel road
to the mailbox at the highway's edge.
No one but us and so much time.
Today my daughter is wearing yellow velour shorts
and matching top, a strip of white tassels
cuts diagonally across her chest.
When she walks ahead, chin in the air,
she looks patriotic somehow —
one of those small baton tossers
marching at the front of an American parade.
At the rifle range we stop to look over the fence:
one-dimensional men lined up side by side,
hearts pinned to their breasts,
and brazen as bull's-eyes. *Where are they?*
my daughter asks, meaning the police
who drive here on Sunday mornings, the trucks
and Jeeps that stampede the field to powdered dust.
Moss perfects and slows our world down.
Wherever we look, the muscled trunks of arbutus
leap from the earth. A kind of balletic orgy.
And it's true, there are other forests
but none can rival in beauty
the forest we walk through
when the day has become too much for us
and the black outlines of human bodies
wait patiently in the shade
of a July afternoon
as though for a firing squad.

## Wheeling through Tuscany

Last night both children dreamed
they flew to the same foreign country,
and the planes they travelled on
were so poorly constructed
they could look down between their feet
and see the world pass beneath them.
They woke broken-
hearted, longing to go back.
And their faces were uncertain
as though haunted by what they could now
only imagine — fields of sunflowers and cyclamen.
They stared at the cereal soggy in their bowls
and said, *It was green there, really green.*
And what I want to know is
should we book a flight today, should we
travel to Tuscany now the children's inner lives
have spilled like Chianti into ours? Small packs on our backs
should we rent bicycles and pedal into
that wet-grape darkness?

# The Fire

Suddenly this boy is too old
for plastic army men dressed in battle fatigues.
After dinner he hangs around the back steps,
bored and indignant and kicking up dust:
why can't he take the raft he's hammered together

into the middle of the bay? We're doing the dishes
when he slouches in. *Can I dig a pit, put rocks around it,
and build a fire?* It's been a wet summer
so we say yes to the fire and the great, green,
unignitable forest. For three days now

we've carried his meals out to where he's hunkered down
at the edge of a pit in a derelict lawn chair —
an old man chewing tobacco and staring
at nothing. Each morning he breathes
life into it and each night douses it with water.

He loves its insatiable appetite, feeds it crumpled
newspapers, broken branches, he cares for
this fire as though it were a lame rabbit
found in the woods. Tonight the indistinct figure
stabs at dying coals, waves

a glowing stick through the dark.
And what does he write across the sky, what blackboard
message after childhood but before girls
dive into his eyes? So much
has been forbidden —

slingshots, firecrackers, deep water.
But for now he is motherless, all crusty
hair and sooty face, a cave-boy
entrusted with something dangerous and
he will not leave it.

# Letter in Flight

*Piano tuner missing over Pacific hanging from*
*thirty-two helium balloons.*
—Japanese transport ministry spokesman


If I have ceased to trust words, who's to blame?
So long I've been riding this wooden crate,
poorly equipped and tossed in the air like a buoyant cup.

The night before my journey
our telephone rang blue as your favourite shirt.
I stopped my ears, wouldn't listen to coast guards
or government officials, their feet buried
deep in the Kanto plain.

You were not watching when I lifted off.
A tangle of strings! I shouted to the crowd,
how pleased I was with my bird's-eye view.

And higher —
the island arcing northward, the Roof of Hokkaido.

From you I took little.
Only the rice cakes you packed in an old biscuit tin,
the wool blanket your brother gave as a wedding gift.

The balloons above are rotund angels,
each one's six metres wide.
You'd think such lightness could carry me
across a thousand copper seas and yet
I've not reached California.

At first I waved my arms at sandhill cranes,
small aircraft, anything that flew
became a friend but now

I long for the beginning and end of a day,
for our daughter, the way she'd hold for a moment
a face in her hands. And you,
sweeping the porch when I returned in the evening
with a bag of small hammers, my tuning forks.

Keiko, I forgive you everything.
For loving too much and then not enough.

On postcards I scribble short prayers
before dropping them into the waves.

The wind pushes like a hammock.

# Giant among Them

### 1

When we were children wading in the sea
one couple after another arrived from Greenock
to settle in the clapboard houses along the beach —
sharp-tongued women whose husbands were not quite
uncles so we called them by the names
already pinned to their size
back in the old country: *Wee Billy, Wee Robert, Wee Hughie.*
Men who had to look up to our six-foot-tall father.
With his thunderous laugh and great appetite
he was a giant among them.
*What do you expect*, they'd say,
*the English didn't suffer during the war.*
Standing beside them, we measured ourselves
against those stunted years —
air raids and rations,
generations of coal dust choking the lungs.
*Your father grew up on a farm, he lived the life of Riley,*
Uncle Billy'd tease after a few pints.
And we'd dangle our feet over Fisherman's Wharf
waiting for the silver dollar he'd slip us
if we didn't disagree.

### 2

Our father told a different story.
How he picked potatoes till his hands bled, as a boy
how he dreamed not of sex or village girls
but of clotted cream, roast beef, and apple pudding.
And German pilots shot like pigeons out of the Yorkshire sky.
Grateful men who worked alongside him in the fields,
their devotion to the führer now spent
peeling turnips, playing whist with his older sisters.

3

Early July and that war's buried on some distant beach.
Our father no longer hungers for anything
heaped on the plate of this world.
At Witty's Lagoon my sister and I sit on a log
watching my son skim his board through low tide.
Again and again riding the same narrow spit of sand.
I wince at his almost-nakedness,
how thin he's become over winter.
My sister's eyes reach as far as the mountains.
*Our father's body*, she says, *the famished frame*
*of someone always looking to the feast beyond.*

## The Meteoron

When my father died I climbed a steep climb.
I stood at the top of a pine-covered mountain
and watched the earth burn.
The sun lit up pilasters and menhirs and I knew then
why my father had gone to the monastery
perched on the magnificent rocks —
to preserve his solitude, for lack of any other solution.
In life he was not a holy man
but in death he planted himself at the top
of a broad rock-shelf with no access
other than a ladder
only he could fold and draw up.
I shouted as far as the Pindus Mountains
but he could not hear me. Finally at peace
my father sang as he hoisted up chickens and sheep,
buckets of water, his daily bread.
I watched him work his nets and winches,
remembering how the heft and weight of things
had always been good in his hands.
It's been years since he stole like a monk into the Meteoron.
Don't ask me what it means —
the fantastic distance
between heaven and earth.
Why we must face a surreal landscape —
needles and sugarloaves, architectures of dizzying blue.
Go now to Trikkala, that city of antiquity
where the finest horses were bred for their beauty and speed.
Do what you must with your own father's death.
I have done what I could with mine.

## The Picnic

I walked down an old logging road at the end of June.
By then only cattle passed through that part of the forest
on their way to a pasture that opened among the trees
like a blast of goodwill. I was fifteen and carried
a sketch pad hoping to spot a deer but spied instead

a man and woman picnicking on a bluff.
Their complete absorption absorbed me completely.
From where I stood it seemed their lips not their words
held the meaning, that their conversation would continue
for weeks or months if only the sun would stay high.

What fixed me to that place was the sound of high wind
like the sound of rushing water, my sudden aloneness
and the fear I'd never get past it. I rested against
a moss-covered stump and when I opened my eyes
they were still talking and laughing, and then the man

shuddered as though a terrible memory had come unlodged.
Have I mentioned they were naked, that the woman
reached over and comforted the man with a tenderness,
even I, shameless voyeur, had to turn from?
A series of soft blows to the heart drew me back

and back again to sketching their profiles, and when
the woman knelt over the man the way a carpenter
will kneel in the shavings at the end of the day —
hands, breath, a flawless plane of wood —
I put down my blunt piece of charcoal.

# A Strange and Terrible Thing

This is the dream:
I'm making love to a dog.
And though I'm troubled by the canine
features of my desire
I choose to ignore
what I know in my passion —
that our coupling is a strange
and terrible thing contrary to nature.
And when the dog rises up on its hind legs
I see it has the body of a man.
Though in every other sense
it's still a dog —
tail and fur and long smooth snout.
The act is without cruelty; we meet halfway,
standing upright, face to face.
And afterwards I feel no shame.
I understand the dog is a vessel containing
the sorrow accumulated in a lifetime.
And I want always to hold in my mind
the human beauty of the dog's face
so I draw a thick frame around it —
a train window retreating
into the distance. And later I wake
aching with a loneliness I had not known
before the dog came to me in the night
and pressed its body against the dark animal of mine.
All day I walk in dumb circles
remembering how the dog bent me down
with paws I can only describe now
as the intelligent hands of love.
And here, in this exhausted light,
I call and call out — *Oh, core of my heart* —
words that mean nothing
but obliterate all else.

## Even the Brilliant Chimpanzees

In the Chinese restaurant we drink
Tsingtao beer and choke down
words, handful by handful.
We grow quiet in the name
of our fervent desires.
Sometimes it is easier to exist

in silence. What other
eloquences have we learned
in two million years?
At Olduvai Gorge someone picked up
the sliver whacked off a rock,
peeled words from the other's

tongue like peeling rind
from a freshly picked melon.
Outside, the streets are ancient
gullies roaming the badlands of Tanzania.
But we do not huddle in wet misery, no, we are
smarter than that, have just enough sense

to come inside where these vermilion
walls hold back the elements
as we try to hold back
primitive emotion. Darling,
we are old, much older
than the grunts and squawks

sprouting from the buds at the end
of our spinal cords, older even
than the dried-up riverbed Leaky discovered—

that forty kilometre gash
in the earth's surface. Tonight
it is your mammalian brain
that bowls me over, that beautiful
cantaloupe ripening beneath your skull.
And if we were to climb up
on the table between us,
go for each other
smelling of ginger root and lime

would the sky
cease pouring its grief
into every crevasse? When it rains
even the brilliant chimpanzees
fold their hands over their heads
in little caps of shelter.

# Acknowledgements

I would like to thank Malaspina College and the Ralph Gustafson Poet in Residency during which time I worked on the final editing of the manuscript, British Columbia's Cultural Services Branch, and the Canada Council for its support during the years of 1998 and 1999. Thanks also to the editors of the following journals in which some of these poems were first published: *Arc, Border Crossings, Canadian Forum, CV II, Descant, Event, Fiddlehead, Grain, The League of Canadian Poets: Vintage 93, 94, 96, 97, & 99, Malahat Review, Poetry Canada Review, Prairie Fire, Prism International,* and *Room of One's Own.*

My sincere thanks also go to the following people: Martha Sharpe for her continued support; Adrienne Leahey, the copy editor we all dream about; Don Coles for his expert advice and close editorial reading of the poems; Derk Wynand and Richard Lemm who taught me so much at the beginning; Linda Rogers for her generosity and friendship over the years; and Terence Young for his love.